Dolphins & Porpoises

Published by Wildlife Education, Ltd.
9820 Willow Creek Road, Suite 300, San Diego, California 92131

ISBN 1-888153-49-0

Dolphins & Porpoises

Series Created by
John Bonnett Wexo

Written by
Beth Wagner Brust

Scientific Consultant
Sam Ridgway, D.V.M., Ph.D.

Art Credits

Paintings; John Francis. **Additional Art: Pages Eight and Nine:** Walter Stuart; **Page Nine: Right,** Walter Stuart and Charles Byron; **Page Seventeen: Middle Right,** Walter Stuart; Activities Art: Bonnie Pilson Kuhn.

Photographic Credits

Front Cover: Brian Parker *(Tom Stack and Associates);* **Pages Six and Seven:** Stephen J. Krasemann *(DRK Photo);* **Page Eight: Left,** Norbert Wu; **Page Ten: Left,** Lee Trail; **Page Eleven: Top,** D. Parer and E. Parer-Cook *(Auscape International);* **Right,** Dr. George Miller; **Page Thirteen: Left,** Bill Curtsinger *(Photo Researchers);* **Upper Right,** Howard Hall; **Middle Right,** Veronica Tagland *(Wildlife Education, Ltd);* **Pages Fourteen and Fifteen:** Howard Hall; **Page Sixteen: Left,** Dotte Larsen *(Bruce Coleman, Inc.);* **Pages Sixteen and Seventeen: Bottom,** Dotte Larsen *(Bruce Coleman, Inc.);* **Page Eighteen:** Elizabeth Gawain; **Page Nineteen: Upper Left,** Art Resource New York; **Lower Left,** Flip Nicklin; **Lower Right,** Karen Pryor; **Page Twenty:** Bruce Coleman *(Bruce Coleman, Ltd.);* **Page Twenty-one: Upper Left,** Doug Wechsler *(Animals Animals/Earth Scenes);* **Middle Right,** Anonymous; **Bottom Left,** Cristina Smith; **Page Twenty-two: Middle Left,** Art Resource New York; **Page Twenty-Three: Upper Right,** Crestina Smith.

Our Thanks To: Hannah Bernard; Steve Leatherwood *(Oceans Unlimited);* Kathy Kangas *(Oceans Unlimited);* Birgit Winning *(Oceanic Society);* Jay Townsend *(Greenpeace);* Roy Allen *(National Marine Fisheries Service);* Scott Trimmingham *(Sea Shepherd);* William Perrin, Ph. D.; Randall Wells, Ph.D. *(Brookfield Zoo);* Pieter Folkens, Ph.D. *(The Oceanic Society);* W. J. Houck; Robert Baracz *(Sea World, San Diego);* Bernd Wursig, Ph.D.; The Earth Island Institute; Rachel Smolker; Elizabeth Gawain; Randall Reeves; William T. Everett; Pak Chin; Susan Chadwick; Paul Brust; Sean Brust; Laurie Bailey Brust; Scripps Institution of Oceanography; Tom Sessions; Joe Selig.

Contents

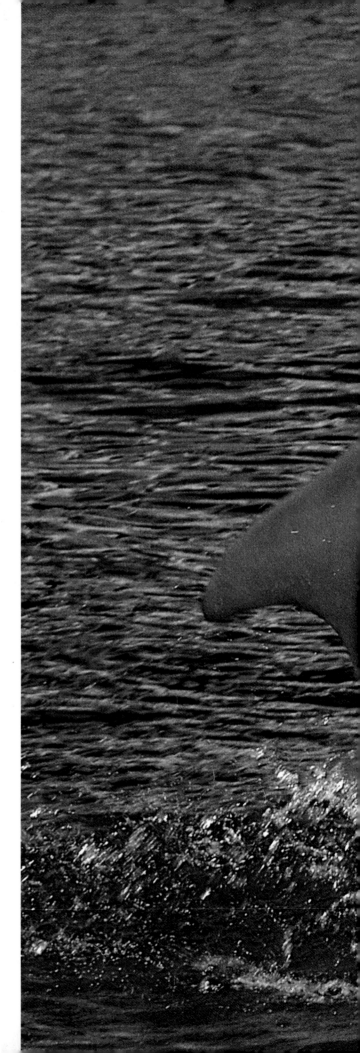

Dolphins and porpoises are popular with everyone. Their lively leaps and built-in grins make them easy to love. And their playful curiosity and cleverness make them fascinating to watch. You never know what a dolphin will do next!

Swift and acrobatic swimmers, dolphins are the mischief-makers of the sea. They *love* to play! And they'll play with almost anything—from feathers to sea turtles to people!

Their more serious cousins, the porpoises, spend most of their time feeding. And they are much more wary of strangers. Unlike dolphins, they keep their distance from boats and people.

Not that dolphins aren't shy, too. But some types are friendlier than others—especially bottlenose dolphins. They seem to want to know everything. And they are surprisingly unafraid of humans. These are the dolphins that you see most often in movies, on television, and in aquatic parks.

Dolphins and porpoises are whales, or *cetaceans* (seh-TAY-shuns). But they are the *smallest* whales in the whole whale family. The largest dolphin is 12 feet long (3.7 meters) and weighs 1500 pounds (680 kilograms)—but some whales are as long as 100 feet (30 meters) and weigh up to 392,000 pounds (178,000 kilograms)!

Like all whales, dolphins and porpoises are *mammals*. They have lungs and must breathe air. They are warm-blooded, with a steady body temperature. And their babies are born alive and feed on milk from their mothers.

Because dolphins and porpoises spend most of their time underwater, they are still somewhat of a mystery. But studies of wild dolphins show that they live in societies, with rules governing all the members. If a dolphin breaks the rules, he or she may be kicked out of the group.

Some scientists think that these outcast dolphins may be the ones that seek out human companionship. But for whatever reason, dolphins have befriended people for centuries. Perhaps that is why people have always felt something special toward them. And perhaps that is why so many people want to protect dolphins and porpoises from fishing nets, pollution, and other manmade dangers. They want to make sure that these delightful animals will be around for centuries to come.

Dolphins can "walk" on their strong tails! They can also do somersaults, body twists, back flips, and side slams.

Bottlenose dolphin

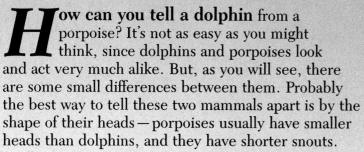
SPOTTED DOLPHIN
Stenella frontalis

H ow can you tell a dolphin from a porpoise? It's not as easy as you might think, since dolphins and porpoises look and act very much alike. But, as you will see, there are some small differences between them. Probably the best way to tell these two mammals apart is by the shape of their heads—porpoises usually have smaller heads than dolphins, and they have shorter snouts.

All together there are 25 kinds of saltwater dolphins, 5 kinds of freshwater dolphins, and 6 kinds of porpoises. Freshwater dolphins are found only in a few large rivers in Asia and South America. But saltwater dolphins and porpoises live all over the world—a few are even found in polar waters. Dolphins do not migrate great distances like large whales. But some do travel hundreds of miles in search of food.

Just one look at this dolphin *fish*, or "mahi-mahi," and you wonder how anyone could confuse it with the dolphin *mammal*. Like all fish, the mahi-mahi is cold-blooded, breathes through gills, and lays eggs. Like other mammals, dolphins are warm-blooded, have lungs and breathe air, and give birth to live young.

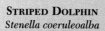
STRIPED DOLPHIN
Stenella coeruleoalba

GANGES RIVER DOLPHIN
Platanista gangetica

The Ganges River dolphin, or "susu" (SOO-soo), is a freshwater dolphin found in India and Bangladesh. Almost blind, the susu uses its long snout to probe for food along the river bottom.

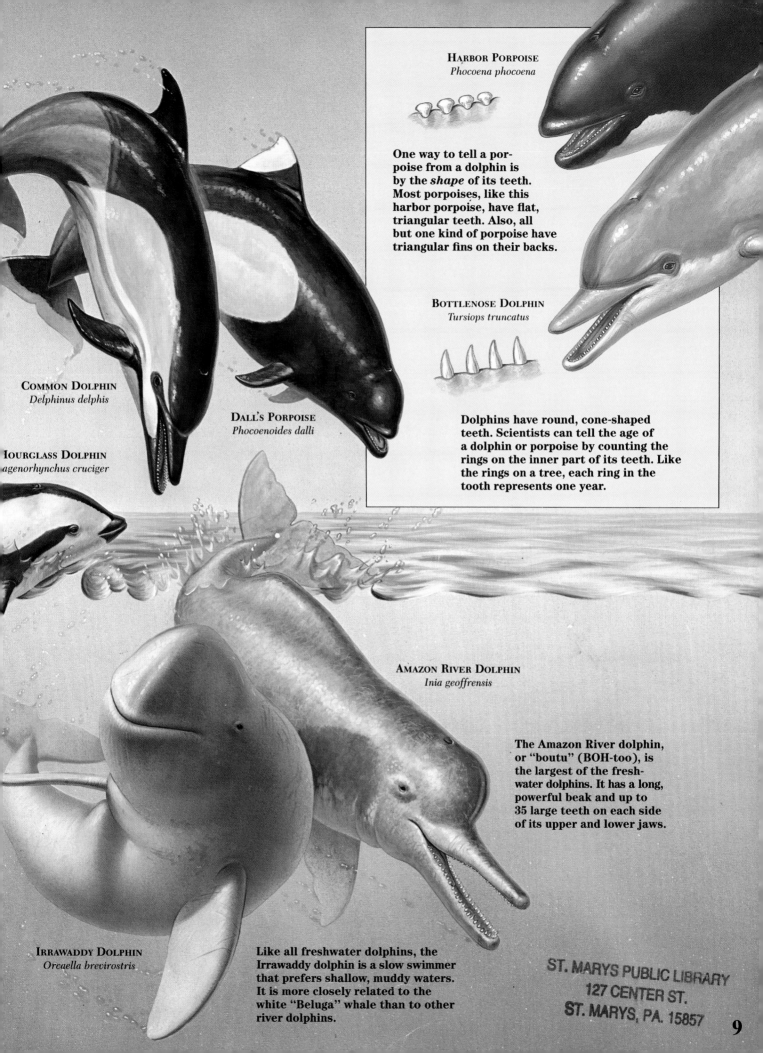

HARBOR PORPOISE
Phocoena phocoena

One way to tell a porpoise from a dolphin is by the *shape* of its teeth. Most porpoises, like this harbor porpoise, have flat, triangular teeth. Also, all but one kind of porpoise have triangular fins on their backs.

BOTTLENOSE DOLPHIN
Tursiops truncatus

Dolphins have round, cone-shaped teeth. Scientists can tell the age of a dolphin or porpoise by counting the rings on the inner part of its teeth. Like the rings on a tree, each ring in the tooth represents one year.

COMMON DOLPHIN
Delphinus delphis

HOURGLASS DOLPHIN
Lagenorhynchus cruciger

DALL'S PORPOISE
Phocoenoides dalli

AMAZON RIVER DOLPHIN
Inia geoffrensis

The Amazon River dolphin, or "boutu" (BOH-too), is the largest of the freshwater dolphins. It has a long, powerful beak and up to 35 large teeth on each side of its upper and lower jaws.

IRRAWADDY DOLPHIN
Orcaella brevirostris

Like all freshwater dolphins, the Irrawaddy dolphin is a slow swimmer that prefers shallow, muddy waters. It is more closely related to the white "Beluga" whale than to other river dolphins.

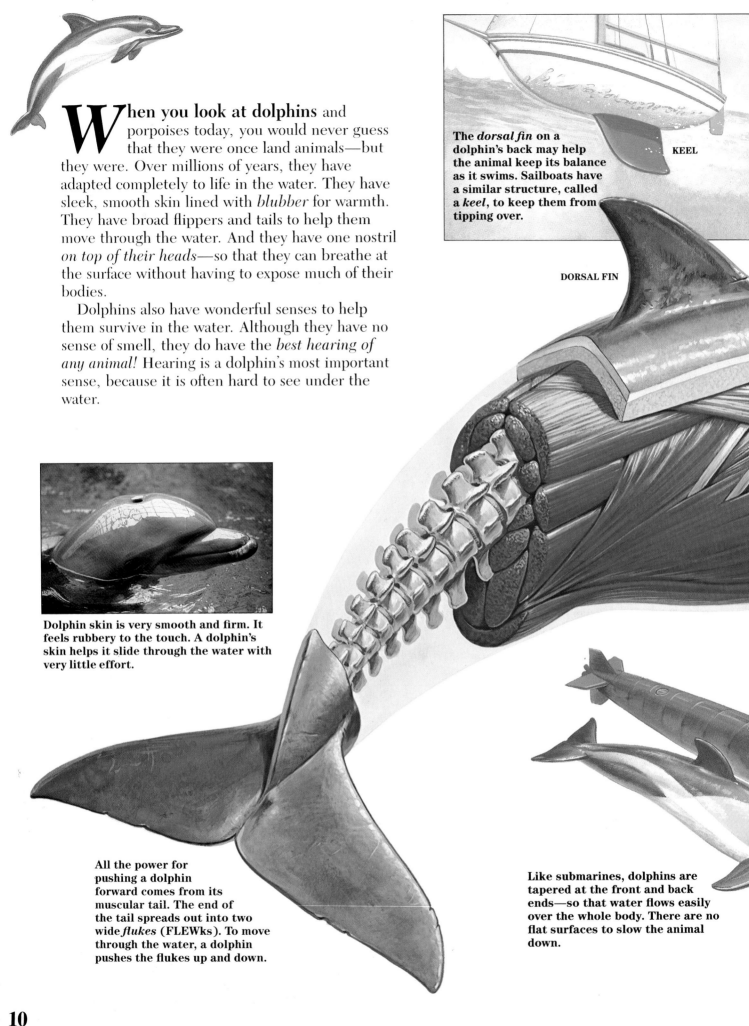

When you look at dolphins and porpoises today, you would never guess that they were once land animals—but they were. Over millions of years, they have adapted completely to life in the water. They have sleek, smooth skin lined with *blubber* for warmth. They have broad flippers and tails to help them move through the water. And they have one nostril *on top of their heads*—so that they can breathe at the surface without having to expose much of their bodies.

Dolphins also have wonderful senses to help them survive in the water. Although they have no sense of smell, they do have the *best hearing of any animal!* Hearing is a dolphin's most important sense, because it is often hard to see under the water.

The *dorsal fin* on a dolphin's back may help the animal keep its balance as it swims. Sailboats have a similar structure, called a *keel*, to keep them from tipping over.

KEEL

DORSAL FIN

Dolphin skin is very smooth and firm. It feels rubbery to the touch. A dolphin's skin helps it slide through the water with very little effort.

All the power for pushing a dolphin forward comes from its muscular tail. The end of the tail spreads out into two wide *flukes* (FLEWks). To move through the water, a dolphin pushes the flukes up and down.

Like submarines, dolphins are tapered at the front and back ends—so that water flows easily over the whole body. There are no flat surfaces to slow the animal down.

Dolphins can dive under the water, but they must always come up again for air. They breathe through a nostril called a *blowhole*. But unlike people, who breathe automatically, dolphins have to *think about* breathing.

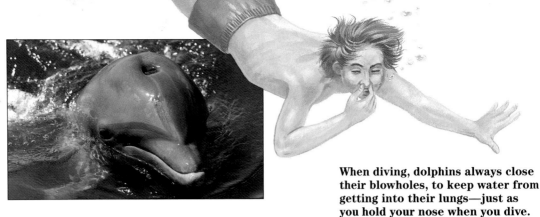

When diving, dolphins always close their blowholes, to keep water from getting into their lungs—just as you hold your nose when you dive. To close its blowhole, a dolphin uses powerful muscles on the top of its head.

Like all whales, dolphins have a clear, jelly-like substance in their eyes that looks like tears. This substance keeps the salt from irritating their eyes as they swim underwater.

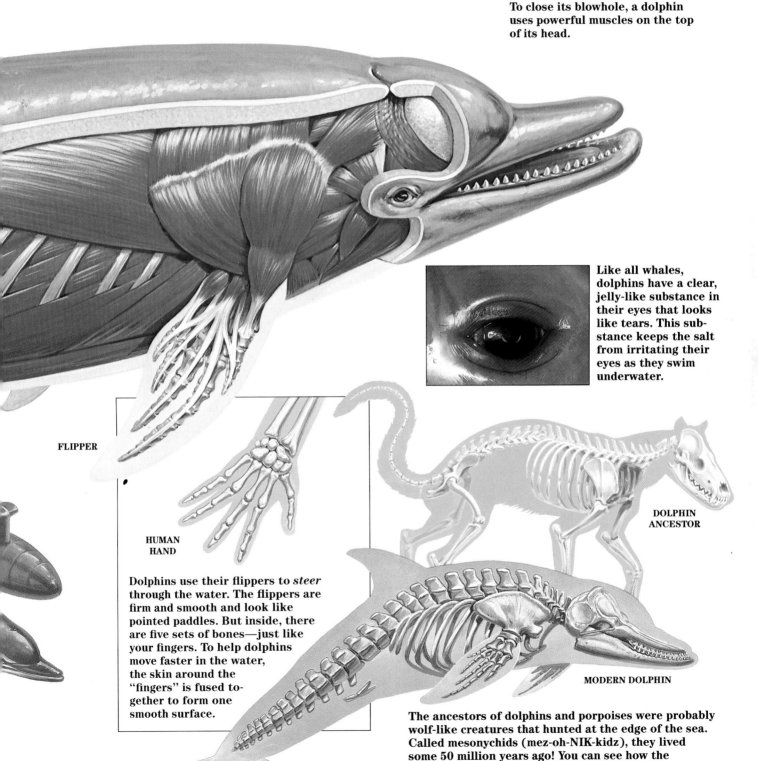

FLIPPER

HUMAN HAND

DOLPHIN ANCESTOR

MODERN DOLPHIN

Dolphins use their flippers to *steer* through the water. The flippers are firm and smooth and look like pointed paddles. But inside, there are five sets of bones—just like your fingers. To help dolphins move faster in the water, the skin around the "fingers" is fused together to form one smooth surface.

The ancestors of dolphins and porpoises were probably wolf-like creatures that hunted at the edge of the sea. Called mesonychids (mez-oh-NIK-kidz), they lived some 50 million years ago! You can see how the forelimbs became flippers over time. And notice that the hindlimbs are now tiny, useless bones behind the dolphin's ribs.

Some dolphins and porpoises feed at night. Others feed during the day. Although fish and squid are their favorite foods, dolphins may also hunt other kinds of prey. Bottlenose dolphins are the least fussy eaters of all. Besides fish, they'll dine on anything from eels and sharks to hermit crabs and worms. This could be why bottlenose dolphins can live almost anywhere and are doing so well!

Dolphins have an extraordinary ability to find food underwater. They use sound waves, or *sonar* (SOH-nahr)—also called *echolocation* (EK-oh-low-KAY-shun). Since sound travels five times faster under water than through the air, sonar is a very effective system. As you will see below, dolphins use their sonar to find food and to spot danger in dark or muddy water.

When feeding at the surface, some dolphins will leap out of the water to catch a flying fish!

If you stood across from a tall building and shouted "hello," a faint "hello" would probably come back to you as an echo.

HELLO! HELLO! HELLO! HELLO! HELLO! HELLO! HELLO!

Dolphins and porpoises use echoes to help them find food—but instead of words, they make a clicking sound. The clicks hit whatever is around them and then bounce back to the dolphins. Dolphins can send as many as *2,000 clicks per second!*

CLICK! CLICK! CLICK!

FISH! FISH! FISH!

Some scientists compare the dolphin's brain to a computer because it can process so many clicks so quickly. *In just one second*, a dolphin can learn all about an object—its size, shape, speed, and direction. A dolphin's sonar is so sensitive, it can detect a fish the size of a minnow from *10 feet away* (3 meters)!

Dolphins often work as a team to catch fish. ① First, they herd a school of fish into a tight group.

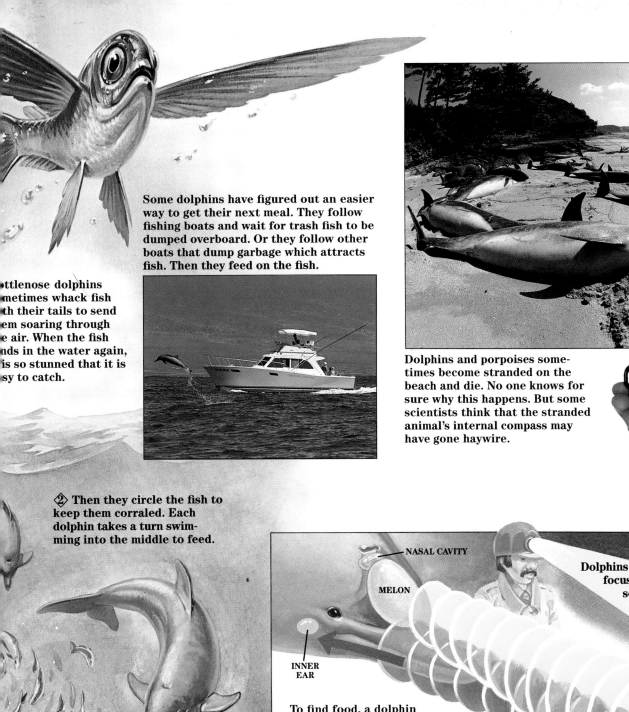

Some dolphins have figured out an easier way to get their next meal. They follow fishing boats and wait for trash fish to be dumped overboard. Or they follow other boats that dump garbage which attracts fish. Then they feed on the fish.

ttlenose dolphins
metimes whack fish
th their tails to send
em soaring through
e air. When the fish
nds in the water again,
is so stunned that it is
sy to catch.

Dolphins and porpoises some-times become stranded on the beach and die. No one knows for sure why this happens. But some scientists think that the stranded animal's internal compass may have gone haywire.

⟨2⟩ Then they circle the fish to keep them corraled. Each dolphin takes a turn swim-ming into the middle to feed.

NASAL CAVITY

MELON

INNER
EAR

Dolphins focus their sonar the same way a miner focuses his flashlight beam.

To find food, a dolphin sends out a series of clicks. The sound starts in air sacs in the nasal cavity. Then it moves forward through a structure in the dolphin's forehead called the *melon*. The echoes from the fish bounce back and travel through the lower jaw to the inner ear.

Once a dolphin catches a fish, it turns it around and swallows it head first! Dolphins have very sharp teeth. But they use their teeth only for grab-bing and holding the fish, not for chewing it.

Spotted dolphins get their spots when
they are adults. Can you tell the young
dolphins from the adults in this picture?

Dolphins and porpoises are social animals. They gather in herds or schools of all sizes. Harbor porpoises usually roam coastal waters in small groups of 2 to 5 members. But deep sea dolphins are seen in enormous herds of 100,000 or more! Still, the basic bottlenose dolphin family consists of about 5 to 10 members, with 2 to 4 adult females and their offspring. Small groups of males swim separately, looking out for each other and hunting together.

Dolphins and porpoises communicate through a mix of sound, body movements, and postures. Above the water, dolphins open their mouths and make creaky-door sounds or high-pitched squeals. Below the water, they make many sounds that are too high for humans to hear.

Dolphin calves stay with their mothers for 3 to 6 years. At birth, they weigh 30 to 50 pounds (13.6 to 22.7 kilograms), and are 35 to 50 inches long (88.9 to 127 centimeters). They are toothless for several weeks.

One way that dolphins communicate with each other is by whistling. They whistle when they are frightened or lonely. They also whine, groan, and clap their jaws. Sometimes they even sound like they are laughing!

16

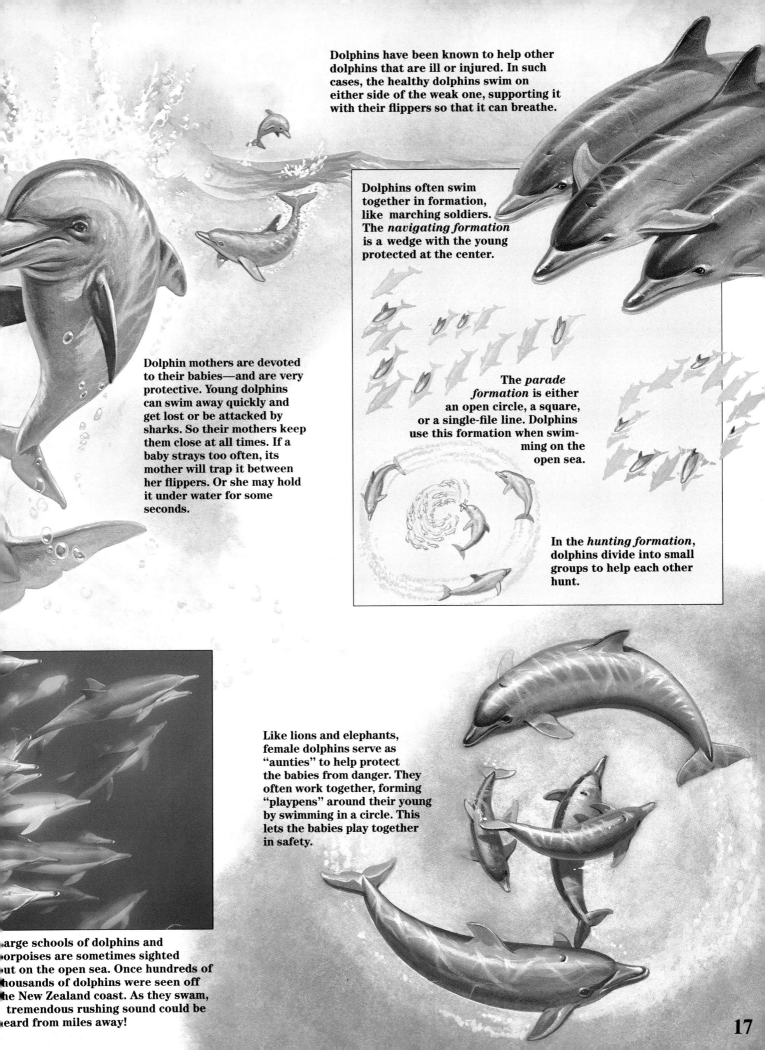

Dolphins have been known to help other dolphins that are ill or injured. In such cases, the healthy dolphins swim on either side of the weak one, supporting it with their flippers so that it can breathe.

Dolphins often swim together in formation, like marching soldiers. The *navigating formation* is a wedge with the young protected at the center.

The *parade formation* is either an open circle, a square, or a single-file line. Dolphins use this formation when swimming on the open sea.

Dolphin mothers are devoted to their babies—and are very protective. Young dolphins can swim away quickly and get lost or be attacked by sharks. So their mothers keep them close at all times. If a baby strays too often, its mother will trap it between her flippers. Or she may hold it under water for some seconds.

In the *hunting formation*, dolphins divide into small groups to help each other hunt.

Like lions and elephants, female dolphins serve as "aunties" to help protect the babies from danger. They often work together, forming "playpens" around their young by swimming in a circle. This lets the babies play together in safety.

Large schools of dolphins and porpoises are sometimes sighted out on the open sea. Once hundreds of thousands of dolphins were seen off the New Zealand coast. As they swam, a tremendous rushing sound could be heard from miles away!

17

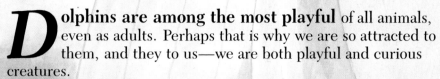

Dolphins are among the most playful of all animals, even as adults. Perhaps that is why we are so attracted to them, and they to us—we are both playful and curious creatures.

Playing is actually a sign of intelligence. And dolphins reveal a lot about themselves through the games they play. They solve problems, tease each other, and show great humor and creativity. Not only do dolphins learn human games quickly, but they also make up their own games and teach them to people. They even seem to scold their human playmates if they don't play correctly!

But mostly, dolphins love to frolic. They leap and somersault out of the water. And they bodysurf through the waves along with human surfers, just for the fun of it!

Most dolphins love to ride and leap in the waves created by ships moving through the water. While riding in these waves, dolphins can go *more than 35 miles per hour* (56 kilometers per hour), without even moving their tails!

In some parts of the world, wild dolphins swim right up to the shore to play with people. But as friendly as these dolphins can be, it's still important for people to be careful when playing with them so that no one will get hurt.

Scientists still have much to learn about dolphins and porpoises. Because dolphins have large brains with many folds, people assume that they are highly intelligent. But so far, there is no scientific evidence that they are any smarter than monkeys.

18

People have admired dolphins and porpoises since the beginning of civilization. This ancient Greek mural was painted *over 3,000 years ago!* It is one of the earliest known examples of dolphins in art.

No one knows why dolphins push people or objects toward the shore, but they have done it many times. During World War II, a group of American airmen were stranded in a raft when two dolphins came along and pushed them toward land.

Dolphins will play with almost anything—balls, feathers, driftwood, seaweed, and even their food when they are full. They also play with other sea animals —turtles, fish, seals, birds, and whales— whether the other animals want to play or not!

Even though dolphins have flippers instead of hands, they still use tools—another sign of intelligence. For example, they use coral reefs as a tool to catch fish. They corner the fish inside the barrier, then dart in to feed.

For thousands of years, people in Brazil have depended on dolphins to help them catch fish. When a school of fish approaches, the dolphin makes a splash in the water. Then the fisherman throws in his net. The fish that don't get caught in the net are eaten by the dolphin.

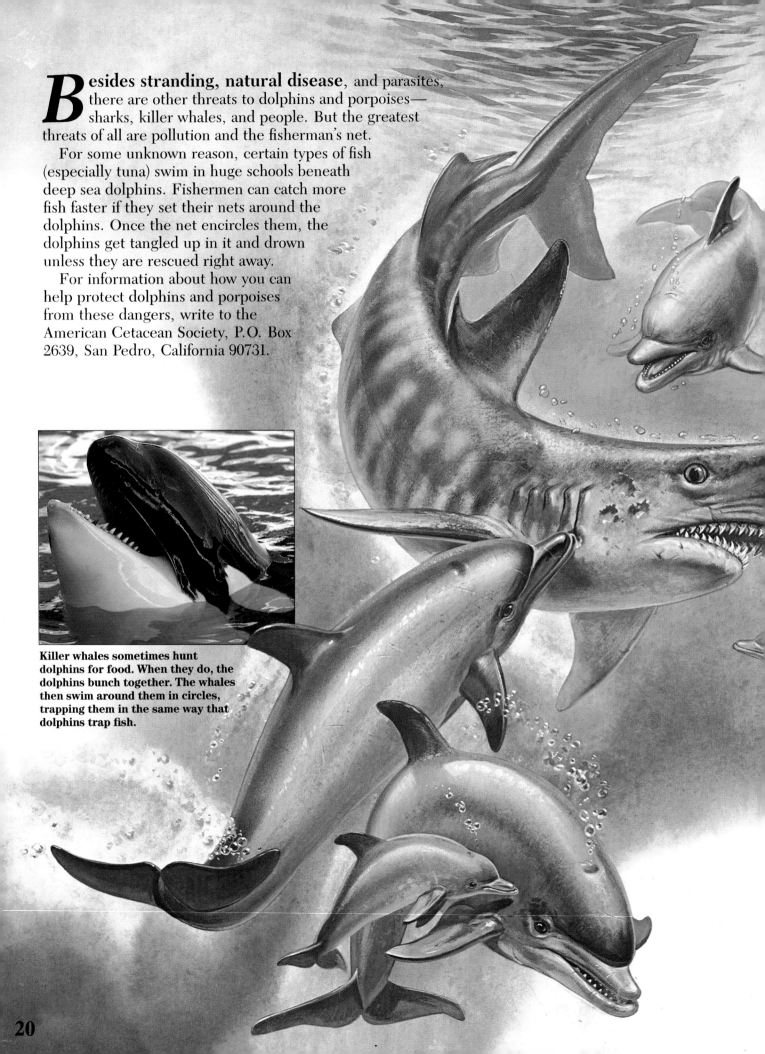

esides stranding, natural disease, and parasites, there are other threats to dolphins and porpoises— sharks, killer whales, and people. But the greatest threats of all are pollution and the fisherman's net.

For some unknown reason, certain types of fish (especially tuna) swim in huge schools beneath deep sea dolphins. Fishermen can catch more fish faster if they set their nets around the dolphins. Once the net encircles them, the dolphins get tangled up in it and drown unless they are rescued right away.

For information about how you can help protect dolphins and porpoises from these dangers, write to the American Cetacean Society, P.O. Box 2639, San Pedro, California 90731.

Killer whales sometimes hunt dolphins for food. When they do, the dolphins bunch together. The whales then swim around them in circles, trapping them in the same way that dolphins trap fish.

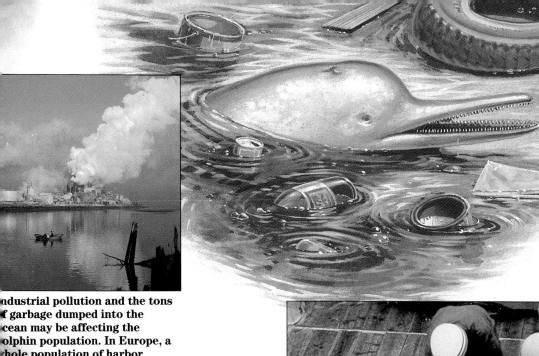

Two of the freshwater dolphins—the susu of India and the baiji (BAY-gee) of China—are close to extinction. There is such tremendous pollution in the rivers where they live that the few dolphins left are barely surviving.

Industrial pollution and the tons of garbage dumped into the ocean may be affecting the dolphin population. In Europe, a whole population of harbor porpoises was wiped out when industrial chemicals were dumped into the sea.

The net used to catch tuna is called a *purse-seining* (SANE-ing) net. When fish swim into the net, a string is pulled at the bottom to trap them inside it. Unfortunately, dolphins sometimes get caught along with the fish.

Sometimes sharks attack young dolphins. When this happens, the adult dolphins quickly surround the shark and take turns ramming its soft underbelly with their hard snouts. Sharks have no bones in their bodies, just cartilage—so it's usually the dolphins that win these battles.

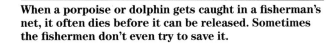

When a porpoise or dolphin gets caught in a fisherman's net, it often dies before it can be released. Sometimes the fishermen don't even try to save it.

WHAT YOU CAN DO!

You can help protect the future of dolphins and porpoises by letting lawmakers know how you feel. Start a letter-writing campaign. Tell your Representative, Senator, and the President how important it is to keep the oceans clean and pollution-free. Ask them not to allow fishermen to kill dolphins just to find more fish. And ask them to urge other nations to pass laws that protect dolphins and porpoises from fishermen's nets. Also, if you live along the coast, volunteer for your local stranding network.

If you ever come across a stranded dolphin or porpoise, here's what you should do:

1) If the animal is on its side, prop it up so that it can breathe.

2) Put wet cloth or paper towels over the body *and* the exposed eye to protect them from sand and sun. Be sure to keep the tail flukes, dorsal fin, flippers, and head wet—because they give off the most heat. Do NOT get water in the blowhole.

3) Call the nearest stranding network or aquatic park for a rescue.

4) If possible, float the animal into shallow water. Again, you *must* keep the blowhole clear. If too much water gets into the blowhole, the dolphin will drown.

ACTIVITIES

Dive into these fun dolphin activities.
Use what you learned about
dolphins to complete the exercises
on these two pages.

A Whale of a Word Puzzle

Answer the following questions about dolphins and porpoises by listing the missing word on a piece of paper. (The number of blanks shows the number of letters in the missing word.) Then look at the first letter in each word you wrote to discover a secret word.

- Dolphins and porpoises are ■■■ - ■■■■■■■, with a steady body temperature.
- They have blowholes on the tops of their ■■■■■.
- Their babies are born ■■■■■ and feed on milk from their mothers.
- Dolphins and porpoises have ■■■■■ and must breathe air.
- Dolphins and porpoises use ■■■■■■■■■■■■, a kind of sonar, to find food.

Answers: Warm-blooded Heads Alive Lungs Echolocation

Off the Wall

Dolphins have appeared in works of art for centuries. For example, the painting above was made over 3 thousand years ago! It is a fresco. That means that it was painted on a wall before the plaster was dry. This fresco and many others showing sea life can be found in the Palace of Minos at Knossos on the Greek island of Crete. See pages 2 and 3 to find out what kind of dolphin is pictured in the ancient fresco. Then try making your own dolphin artwork to cover a wall of your room. Use paint, crayon, or felt pen to create a dolphin mural on butcher paper.

Those A-Mazing Dolphins

Help the two divers swim through the maze of dolphins. Show them the path that will take them back to their boat.

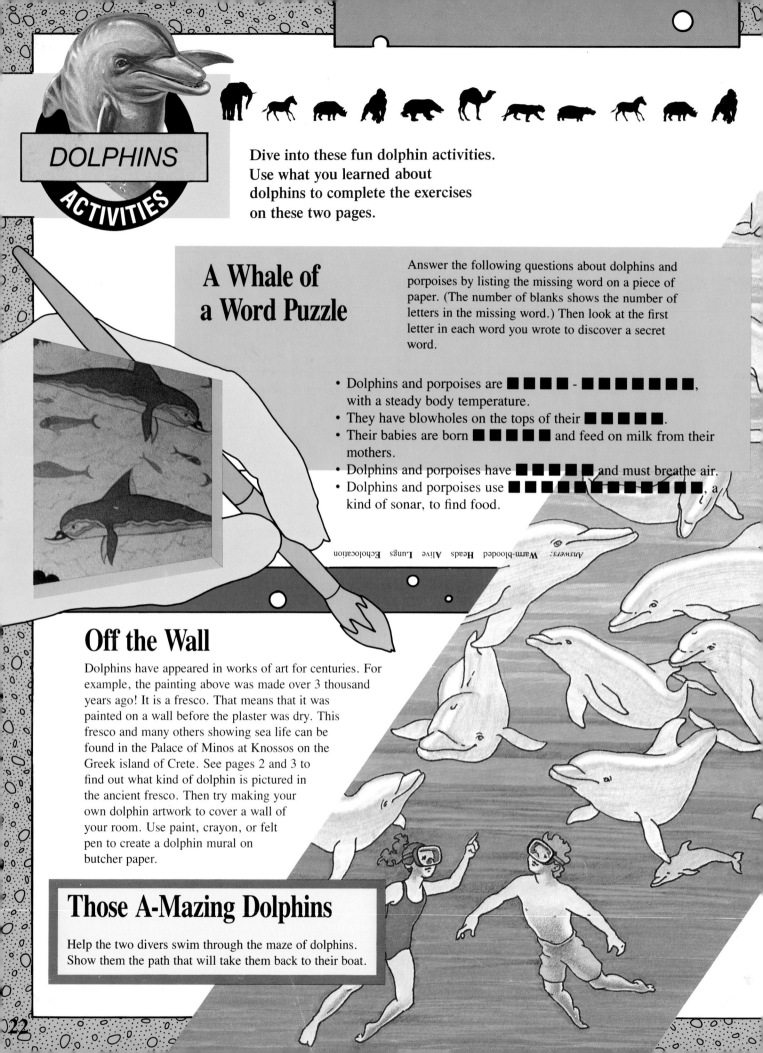

Navigate Like a Dolphin

You have learned that dolphins may have built-in compasses. You can build your own compass. First, tie a string around the middle of a bar magnet. (You can find a bar magnet at a hardware store.) Let the magnet hang from the string. One end of the magnet will point to the North. Place a piece of tape around this end. (If you are unsure which end is pointing North, ask an adult to help you.) Mark your starting point with tape. Use your magnet to navigate through this course:

1. 5 steps North
2. 3 steps East
3. 1 step North
4. 6 steps West
5. 4 steps South
6. 2 steps East
7. 2 steps South
8. 1 step East

Where did you end up? Now plot a course of your own to follow.

Pin a Dolphin on a Friend!

You can create a dolphin pin to give to someone you know. (Make an extra one to wear yourself.) Follow these directions. You will need: scratch paper; thin, white cardboard (such as an index card); crayons; a safety pin; masking tape; a paintbrush; and white glue.

1. Sketch dolphin shapes on a piece of scratch paper. Look at the pictures of dolphins on pages 2 and 3 for ideas. Make your dolphins about 3 inches (8 cm) long. When you create one that you like, cut it out. Then trace an exact copy of it on a piece of thin, white cardboard.

2. Color the front of your dolphin with crayon. Then use a piece of masking tape to attach a safety pin to the back of your dolphin. Spread white glue over the entire back, covering all of the masking tape but not the safety pin. Let this dry overnight.

3. The next day, spread white glue over the front of your dolphin pin. Let it dry overnight. The glue will be clear when it dries. To make your pin shinier, add more glue layers. Let the glue dry between each layer.

TRACE

COLOR

SPREAD GLUE

WEAR!

Read More About Dolphins

The Way of the Dolphin by Dr. Michael Fox. Washington, D.C.: Acropolis Books, 1981.

Explore the natural habitat and behavior of dolphins. Read about the birth of a dolphin and its dramatic escape from killer whales. Discover how these lively mammals play with a fisherman and his son. For older students.

Now I Know Dolphins and Porpoises by Sharon Gordon. Mahwah, New Jersey: Troll Associates, 1985.

If you are a new reader, you can read this one to yourself. Learn about playful dolphins and porpoises. Enjoy the colorful pictures. Compare bottlenose dolphins and porpoises.

Dolphins: Our Friends in the Sea by Judith E. Rinard. Washington, D.C.: National Geographic Society, 1986.

Read about dolphins and other toothed whales. Learn about the differences between life in the wild and life in captivity. Find out what scientists and others have learned about these fascinating mammals. Share the colorful photographs with a friend.

Index